van der Goes, Hugo. *The Fall of Man.*
15th Century, Kunsthistorisches Museum, Vienna

They Are Not People

A Novel By:

Michael Bookout

2020

CONTENTS

Introduction:

I do not like to give time or energy to evil, but a name continues to be spoken in the common marketplaces I frequent. This named individual, a mere man, is said to have financially bankrupt twenty or so countries within my lifetime and he is of a consort to destroy my country as well.

Indeed, if this number of wrecked states is in any portion correct, and that one man alone is responsible for these acts of malice then we know this frail little man is possessed of demonic spirits. For no person could have this great effect working alone.

This statement seems comical in this hour of human history even to myself who lives in Sacramento, California, the city that does not support my art.

But I so very much assure you this powerful earthman is possessed as he, George, has chosen demonic entities for friends for this day and for his life's eternal associations.

Part I

I just received my blood report by phone and the doctor was laughing lightly as he was amazed at the health status at age sixty-six. Exercise is the answer. Daily working out with weights, with time swimming, jogging, stretching and yoga at Julie's studio. Hot yoga to be precise and hot Pilates. Fun. Exhausting. Exhilarating. As good as food as I can find to eat and mental exercising. Emily Dickinson the poet for breakfast as well as Anna Swir and Rilke with his book "Letters to a young Poet", Pablo Neruda (but not so much anymore since he has become a 'hip' poet for our time which sort of takes the mystique out my quiet, secret times with him alone on my couch in the early mornings) and, Rumi as well.

Laurie texted me a furtive message yesterday morning and Dawn a happy, bold one, and Kerith a super positive child of Mother Earth, all wanting to know how I was getting along. During this issue with a world pandemic. All three are professional yoga instructors at Julie's studio. I was flattered that they would be thinking of me and my well-being considering we, earth inhabitants, are riding an ever-rising tide of a flu virus. I love my yoga sisters.

And the very best way to begin every day is to stand in the shower and turn on the hot water and then when the water begins to heat, step out and dry off: summer fall winter spring. Shave if you must, powder and cologne a bit. Dress in loose clothing, pour a cup of caffeinated tea, lit at least one candle, walk to your seat, the seat or couch you use only and ever for the big morning event.

Around your seating place are your books, your other reading publications such as magazines and writing materials with a pad of writing papers. You are to begin reading our most spiritual books. You may pray. After twenty minutes or so you write what is called a 'gratitude list' of the ten things in your life you are most thankful for. You may write more than ten. You then write these words in successive order: Emotion, Mental, Spiritual, Physical, Dreams. Behind/below each of these words write how you feel about YOUR five categories. Example: Emotion: happy. Mental: focused. Etc... writing your Dreams, you save for last and if you remember what you dreamed about and write a brief description or, write nothing. There is more to this morning writing exercise and I will illiterate them in a PowerPoint presentation the next time I lecture in your city with Sparkle, my invisible dog.

Next you open one of two books or both, one to follow the other. A large portfolio book of the universe. Full color. You can find these books, as I have found several in the Salvation Army bookshelves under science. They will be of minimal cost. (I would buy everyone who asks for one to get you started but then I would not have the money to feed Sparkle who it seems has an infinite appetite). Big dog. Big appetite.

To note: For charitable organizations to shop with or donate money or time for, the Salvation Army is by far, the most frugal with your donated monies of alllllllllllllllllllllllllllllllllll ! those other clever hawkers vying for your hard earned dollars.(See the chart below; You decide.)

In addition: to look at pictures of the Milky Way and knowing that there are one billion stars in this star constellation and knowing there are billions of galaxies in the known universe really puts you in the right frame of spirit when you find yourself up against an enormous encounter such as having lost your hair brush.

Your other book is one of poetry. Hopefully you have several/many poetry books. This adventure will give you insight into the minutia of the human soul as it has been examined in every and all its dimensions and in every language. And if you are one who doesn't believe you have a soul then why would you waste your time reading poetry? I mean really…

You then may indulge in the beauty of fine art works from the fine artisans of human recorded existence of the past twelve thousand years. Gilded plates of gold decorated porcelain. Egyptian temples. Fine furniture. Headdresses carved to venerate potentates. Murders and liars these rulers may be, and yet in life you are often to make decisions to overlook and to give what is called a 'blind eye' to in order that you may see beyond the rubble of the battle field to appreciate the sunset, purple skies, the unique orange glow of it all.

The above exercise is called the Golden Hour and if you begin your every day with this or, at the very least, visualize the categories you will have for yourself an exciting sixty minute uninterrupted hour to revive your mental, spiritual and bodily engines. Or, if you so choose, shoot an illegal narcotic into your veins: this will give you at a minimum 'fools hour', maybe more.

And now onto the difficult part of our story:

And just when things were rolling along so very easily, Men in high places of low, amoral gutter dwelling residences dreamed of schemes and viruses to destroy the American economy and America altogether. Some women have cast negative thoughts as well into these purposes; perhaps, many.

Chapter I

They Are Not Human

They have been dreaming all the while and contriving. The very wonder that America was born to and of a Republic is none too miraculous. A cursory study of the 'rebels' those who wanted to be free of British rule took on in a direct hand to hand, eyeball to bayonet confrontation the most advanced army in the world and defeating them is something every human who has ever entered a place of bets, bluffs and loss or win of monies, a place of gambling would have bet the house on the British armies crushing the residents of the America's, their claim of ownership, Britain's, colony.

First the Separatists sailed away to separate themselves from the harsh, cruel British rule then others followed. History of this exodus from Europe and the characters as well as the activities of this period and up to the signing of the Declaration of Independence is well recorded.

This book you are now reading will not be an easy one to digest. It will be graphic which does not mean sexually explicit per se. I will be sharing about transcendental meditation, out of body experiences, inner dimensional coexisting, my political and sociological beliefs, alien encounters and many other topics. In all I might not write another paragraph. But then again…

It is more challenging to me that people do not believe in the definition of 'evil' than people who think I am silly for believing in evil. There is the book The Exorcist and the author, in the introduction section of his book made three claims of evil happenstances that have occurred of people who, in his opinion, have turned their wills to Satan and who have committed atrocities against innocent people. This was the author's effort to convince you that there really is a devil.

I read only that section of the book when it first was published, and I thought I need not read further.

FYI ... There is a monastery in Italy with the theme of being a school to arm priests how to "exorcise" demons from persons. The person who narrated the book written about the monastery says that most priests who are called upon to perform exorcisms experience mostly benign encounters not directly involving spirits which for fun can turn little girls on their heads. And then there are those encounters which a human can observe which it is better not to write about. At least not myself.

I assume my intense searching for all things spiritual came from both my mother and my father. My mother was baptized Catholic and an ardent believer and my father was born into not such a pictorial way of stain glass cathedrals and chanting and colorful vestment choir wearers. His was more of the DNA education from his father, a full born Cherokee and it is said his wife and my father's mother was one half Cherokee and yet I have no way of verifying this about her. And for his connection my father referred to The Great Spirit which is another name given to the name god. And you may be aware that persons who live close to the earth, i.e... tribal persons are highly telepathic. Nice birthday gift dad; gee, thanks!

B. Small town boy seeks knowledge.

When I was a child growing in Fresno California, I pulled a book off my mother's paperback bookshelf and hopped the fence to go sit under a honeysuckle bush to read about St. Francis of Assisi. Ironically, the bush was attached to the fence of my grade school's baseball diamond area on the third base side. I was terrible at sports pretty much and had I been a star of the game, the historical wanderings of St. Francis and his teachings I believe have served me much better in life.

At some other times I have been mentored by persons past and present. I quickly latched onto Gandhi and Jesus and at some point while in my bedroom hallway my grandmother gave me a book and said "This is your book." and walked back into the kitchen of her San Francisco apartment where I was staying an elongated stay as my mother was very ill and could not manage me. And standing there as a child with no explanation why, I held in my hand the biography of, in the end, a very strange enigma of a person. The book was one of those old books that had come from another country as the pages you may know of this time had been cut one by one from each other as the pages had been glued so that they may not get wet in passage.

I kept this book with me for many years often sleeping with it under my pillow and constantly reading from it.

This is not my subtle way of trying to let you know I am a saint for I tell you "I ain't!" I often said that I am as close to a popes and spiritual giants as the east is from the west.

In fact anyone who tells you they are a saint or a prophet they more than likely are trying to make a profit of your ignorance as so deep you are wanting to believe in anything other than your boring life and the fact that you are in a non-fulfilling relationship and making every effort to find a new movie or relive an old one that captured away your emotions to the forever kingdom castle, that is, until you went out into the parking lot to drive away in a car that the rent for such a vehicle comes round far to early each month.

I suppose I am trying to set a little credibility for myself before I continue writing more. For what I tell you more is neither fact nor is it fiction. That is, if you believe you are the only person on this planet and how wonderful it is that you know everything and anything that a person might bring to you that is new or different from your station of wisdom then you can readily reject it. We the seven billion plus are so happy for you.

I know you do not know that I talk to plants so I will not bore you with this detail of my fern communication life until later. I once told my father that plants have emotions. And he laughed. I then took a small potted fern and placed it next to our stereo. I positioned the ferns branches so that they faced the window and their backside was to the stereo speaker. In just two days the fern branches had turned to the stereo speaker which my daddy did play all day that of soft jazz or classical music and the station playing Frankie.

And here it is later, and I will tell you that I do communicate with plants. I do not know what language they are speaking but my, my, those guys really do buzz along at a frantic pace. It is for me very much like sitting in an authentic Mexican restaurant and listening to persons speaking Spanish; I have no idea what they are saying but as they smile and nod their heads to me, their arms and hands go flailing with great expanse and their bodies sway with exaggerated momentum and their bodies arch fore and aft coupled with the up and down of volume in what they are speaking and at the rapidity at which they talk I can pretty much fill in the gaps as to what they are communicating.

And what I have over the years understood of plants and what they are communicating to one another is that they are very busy about their lives and it is so very important to them. And if I do stand among them, they are not in any way offended by my presence, nodding their leaves and petals to me as I am feeling so very blessed to be a part of their communion.

And insects? Well, good luck getting them to communicate with you. I think their community is so very wary of how many of their tribe has been crushed and poisoned by humans and their carcass pinned with long metal spikes to the walls of the 'insect collector's' trunk display case.

And yet after trying so many years to talk with insects, flying or crawling I did communicate with (and I think it must have been a beetle...I only remember it, Her, having a very hard shell she carried as a protective shelter). And she did indeed give so very little attention to me and I was aware she had this "attitude" which was none to pleasant. She probably got back with her tribe and told them she had talked to 'one of them' and how so incredible ignorant I was of understanding their thoughts about life. But this part I just imagine. I have no evidence.

And before we close this section of our story out I would like you to know that animals, mammals and sometimes birds are way more receptive to communicating with you than you had not never wanted to know before.

It is so a bittersweet journey I take to the local zoos. My poor friends. Locked for a torturous eternity behind bars. Had they been 'wheel men' in an armed robbery of a feed store I might not have so much compassion. Some I talk to are literally crazy. Can you understand?

They are one-minute flying free in Madagascar then suddenly taken from the fragile safety they have taken as a normative and, find themselves in cages evermore. And this would be bad enough but then they live the remainder of their hours being stared at by groups of grubby school kids with striped shirts and ice cream flowing down their wrists and arms and often antagonized by these brats with chants and being pelted with shelled peanuts.

I try encouraging them from the bars that separate us and chained linked fences which pen them in. I tell them I love them, and I am so very sad for them. My only claim to this reality is whenever I am invited to go into the home of a person for the very first time Little Fuzzy or whatever the cat's name is comes directly up to me, rubbing upon my leg and wanting to be held. Without fail, the owner of this furry family friend says "God! That is amazing! Little Fuzzy never goes up to strangers...she always hides."

etc.:

We do everything to find love or, to compensate for not having much, if any. I often find myself wandering around as if in a state of cosmic dust, my internal particles just sort of staying together because they have nowhere else to go.

Lou has this trouble as well. Being entrepreneurs both we have this inner voice asking us continually if we are doing the right thing. And what is the right thing? We are asking ourselves if we have a worth? ...a value or purpose? As friends we tend to see the best in both of us. Ah, and just below the surface, the volcano of self-doubt, self-recrimination is broiling. We both say we do waste about ten percent of our business day doing low priority tasks. And yet persons' who are not people are running at full speed even in their sleep. Planning, Plotting, Delegating. Dismissing and crushing "the little people" such as ourselves. Therefore, they are successful.

I must imagine Jeff Bezos of Amazon. What must go through that boy's head from moment to moment. You could easily have a best seller on Amazon if you could record every bit of thought Mr. Bezos thought in a single twenty-four-hour period. But not about his sex life as the universe does greatly frown upon what it comprehends to be sacred and secret. Porn is commerce and is neither sacred nor obviously not secret, just so you know the difference.

To Have a Friend

The word all over is that this person and that is a 'friend'. What I wish to know is where friendship ends and where it began? For Lou and me it began about eleven o'clock one evening when I was cleaning his former fathers-in-law's office. There was Lou analyzing stocks for his family's net returns. I remember thinking when I first introduced myself and he to me that there was something not true about his person as his essence of kindness was all too apparent. And night after night five days per week there he would be transfixed in front of his monitor calculating. A quiet acknowledgement of civility grew between us and in the brief moments of excusing myself for interrupting him that I may get his trash can and empty the days refuse we would begin to reveal ourselves to each other about job, family and activities. And at times I would take the time and sit in one of his receiving chairs as the conversations began taking more than an impromptu greeting as I moved along to the next desk for more trash.

In time I found his general personality was truly not strained and his genuine kindly persona was just that: kind.

It has been over thirty years since we had first met and developed what is a true, real friendship. Children and sharing about their lives with someone who also has children allows both persons to understand that you both have much at stake in this race through life.

Business and the upwards and downwards of national and personal financial responsibilities and reaction to such.

Lou and I have had the 'walk down the beach' conversations for more times than can be numbered. It would not surprise me if we are the ones to have left two ruts in the road. My walking on his left side where his hearing is better.

Our talks always ensue when I go to his home and release a few, agitated, balled up statements which he immediately interprets that I am confused, troubled about some topic and I need to have a good talking through.

This is a friend; a good listener, non-judgmental and one who offers sage answers dotted with anecdotes and with a few personal stories of his own. You leave the presence of your friend cleansed, and though your problem you shared with him is no doubt still there you know you can go it one more day.

A friend is also someone who thinks of you with concern when you are not with them and one who only wishes you wellness. This is a friend. Acquaintances are ones who wish you well but do not ever consider giving you a birthday gift. Adversaries wish only for your destruction as those who fit into the ranks of: They are not People.

And there Lou is minding his own business going about his business providing for his family and there they are the Masters of the Universe, so called, plotting to bring he, Lou, his family and friend me, all under some kind of servitude, slavery or to certain death in the end.

They are called more than Masters of the Universe; Demons, servants of Satan, the Secret Six, The Secret Seven, The Illuminati...choose which door you wish, In the end you get a hell on earth, that is….but of course, unless they deem you to be one of theirs.

Chapter II

Savant or Not

I am alright, and ok, being a savant. I came across it innocently enough. Fresno, California, I was eleven years old; I had just arrived home from the hospital, and with a two-week fever, my parents agreed to a, if you will, Hail Mary penicillin shot. I was injected with a very long needle and I wince at this day to my feelings as a child looking at this long syringe and to know it was to be jabbed into my butt. Owwweee!

And later, propped up on pillows in my bed a Catholic priest entered my bedroom. My mother and father were there, my mother wearing a grey dress in the middle of a warm summer afternoon and my father mysteriously there and not at work, in his business suit. "Mother," I said "why is the priest here?" My mother said "Oh, he just wants to give you an extra blessing," and then passed out from the room a tissue up to her eyes and nose. And then there was a prayer in Latin and then the pastor dipped a wafer into a container of wine, and I took it in my mouth.

I was told to rest. At some time, as many times before, I began vomiting. My parents took me and cleaned me and put me in clean dressing and told me to wait in the living room of our very small house as they cleaned the vomit and changed the bed sheets.

Something took hold of me, and even as a small child I remember how strange my behavior seemed to me as I began running in circles and making an animalistic sound, grunts or more like moans. At one point I dropped to the floor and continued with these noises and began rolling and thrashing on the carpet. And then, I stopped and then I stood. I felt something was happening inside me for which an eleven-year-old child had no words for. I do call this the 'ice crystal conversion'. Inside my body it was as if all my cells had become frozen. It both burned a bit and tingled. This feeling was momentary.

Approximately fifty years later, having stuffed my childhood memories as far away from my consciousness as I could, I was driving on the freeway when on the radio a woman was giving an interview about the book she had written and this was about savants. And as she spoke, she mentioned Mozart the composer and how at an early age he contracted a fever to the point of death and then made a recovery.

This story jelled my memory the crystal conversion for as the author continued she explained that of the savants she wrote about all had had a two week fever/ illness of some sort and this had brought them to the point of death and against all prayers of mourning the children, all the savants to be, recovered. This, for whatever reason of nature is the gateway into savant-hood.

My first display of being a servant was while sitting in my eighth grade math class the teacher, with chalk, had written a long algebraic problem across the entire board and when she had finished I called out the answer to the problem. The teacher as if she had been hit with a rock from behind turned on her heels and said to me "How did you know this is the answer?" And as she turned so did every head of every student turn and stare to my face. I loved this, being a middle child, I desired all the attention I could receive. I especially remembered the girl I was secretly in love with, a dark-haired Latina/Caucasian who smiled warmly at me.

How I did know this answer I did not know. I, for all my years, have struggled greatly with the sciences and maths. And yet now it had become an everyday thing while at one point I could tell you the exact minute on the hand of a watch without looking, I could tell you how many pages were in a book without having been told or having had counted them and I could tell you how many individual figures up to and under two thousand were represented, say on a decorative wall pattern and the figures could be circles or squares or rectangles in random positioning, the same circumference or dissimilar to every other one. For me this was quite satisfying and quite wonderfully fun.

Interesting, many savants are 'challenged' they need constant help in completing a day. For the few others such as the math dude interviewed by David Letterman a television talk show host whose few minutes with the math dude is recorded on You Tube, the math dude tells about his two week illness and filled me in on other facts about savants. For myself as I said my abilities are quite fun, I do not take any credit for their display in the human entity. As I always say "It's a God thing". Others seem boastful.

Part II

Curious, do you not think, former chairman of China, Chairman Mao spent his time inventing torture techniques to be used upon humans. As Stalin and any and every other monster, Mao was responsible for more pain and suffering upon humanity than can be calculated.

And yet, one million Chinese persons make, as it were, a religious trek to the place of Mao's birth annually.

And then there are tours you may take this very day in Siberia where a guide will take paying visitors through the Stalin death camps and tell in intricate detail the gruesome tortures and the hellish life style of those poor millions of Russians who were herded into these camps to labor and to die all at the whim of one possessed by spirits of which I have earlier related.

And let us not raise our hands to tell of our time visiting London where you as well took one of many tours you can pay for to visit the places the decapitated bodies of women were found the work of none other than Jack the Ripper.

Ah yes, something very wrong of this: ya think?

PART III

Now class, and to remember, there are three levels of alien intervention.

A) Government disinformation.

B) Human hoax (and now with all things digital and there is no limit to humans and their parameters of trickery.

C) Welcome the Alien Beings

These three categories balance out into an almost perfectly defined three parts presentation. It will be for you to decide which would be what. And now of course that AI (artificial intelligence) is resident here, it will be all but impossible to separate truth from almost truth to almost no truth to sans truth.

You realize that it is now of the proper temperament to address aliens as Alien Beings. This retrofit-negative fit of the human mind has been defined by Crowd Woke the champions of all that is Right and Proper in today's dialogue and with its every step and in every way commandments torn day by day from the page releases of PC Central Advisory Committee of Detention Enforcement and Deportation. Have a nice day.

#One: Would you know that there really are aliens who have been visiting planet earth when once it settled down from its frothing cauldron in the billions of years it took to achieve its current day's maturity?

Oh yes. And there is more than just a toy box full of information and artifacts left to jumble thru in discovering these. And as related at first, some information is false, some true.

#Two: The eight systems of the human genus: For sure Beings, alien, are curious about the miracle of the eight biological systems of the human species. It is as if each body system conspires with the seven other systems to help provide its own miraculous system to function to its own fullness as it in turn interacts with seven systems to help provide for the overall good of the eight systems while each of the remaining seven systems are of their own invention interacting perfectly with every other system to work in full miraculous cohesion.

#Three: Yes, there is One mind, an interactive mind, which secures, controls, and directs the entire universe and all creation to miraculously interact with all and every other portion of that creation. Protons for example in equal and opposite directions traveling through space when one revolves in on direction and then changes course to revolve in the opposite direction somehow signals to the other proton which was following in exactly the same rotating direction then knows (somehow) to reverse its direction to be in cohesion with the first proton. This is a known quality of the proton, provable and is in some way detailed in Einstein's theory of quantum mechanics for which Einstein himself said of the mimicking protons that this event is: "Spooky".

Part IV

The Rabbit Hole/ down and through to the other side.

If indeed Beings, aliens are here interacting with the human species in the form of Shape shifters or Lizard people what is their end all goal? Their mission? Their purpose? To merely observe and not to manipulate the human species for some reason of their own. Are they here to have sexual intercourse with women to impregnate them as it does say in the Jewish bible in the book of Genesis? I mean, why did they not impregnate the young Angelina Jolie who was one of the earth's most perfect physical specimens of her day so that she might produce multiple children?

And the story goes that in American current culture to come of age of fifty years old this is thought to be a very big tiding. This myth of championing the trials of life and arriving to the age of fifty was to be honored in the early years of humanity when life expectancy was perhaps thirty maximums.

And so to carry on the arcane tradition of 'having achieved' I prepared myself for my memorial birthday and when that day arrived I drove from my home to the mountains to a forest area my friends in high school and in college hiked and camped.

Not being inclined to the incline of the mountain scape nor the thinness of the mountain air I sat down three quarters of the way to my destination ridge where I would go to meditate and to bring in the new half of a decade. I was no match for my youthful energies and I realized that I was not in physical condition enough to climb any further up greatly depressed and disappointed when along a small service road came driving a small worker vehicle and two mountain men rangers who were angled to go on higher and I asked them if I might ride in the back cab to the ridge of my wanted destination. They said for insurance reasons they were not allowed to have pedestrian passengers but they made for me an exception and when they had driven the length to the ridge I tapped on the roof of the vehicle and they stopped allowing me to proceed along the ridge on foot.

Off the road just a bit so that another vehicle or persons could not see me I crouched down among some bushes and stared blankly across the wide gorge on this mild summers day and let my mind drift above the massive tree tops for the miles of space before me.

And then, not long after I arrived, I notice something moving on the floor of the gorge which seemed metallic or a shiny plastic shape, catching the noon day sun. Slowly it moved, and though it was at least a mile down the gorge I could make out a rectangle structure that I estimated to be two football fields across and as it moved ever so slowly, silently it came from without the trees to the approximate length of two football fields in length.

I perceived this rectangle shape to be a Being, Alien craft, and though the distance from which I was situated I could see that the surface was not smooth on the craft but as if it had an uneven structure. And as I looked on with amazement wondering what? I sat very still holding my breathing to a minimum not wanting to give myself away. For I had read to this point in my life and read that aliens do delight in taking humans aboard their ships and probing humans with hot instruments looking for what it was they wanted to investigate.

And as I sat and watched the vehicle moving for about a minute and one half it suddenly stopped, and I gasped inwardly. An though I was a mere spec on a mountain side covered over a bit by brush I was very well aware that Beings do communicate with telepathy and if I have tried to relate anything in this writing it would not be any stretch to understand that I am attuned to telepathy in the ways you have read or seen or heard or experienced yourself as it is quite evident that all humans are interconnected at a telepathic level and so are Beings, alien.

I have never been so disturbed nor terrified even above the time my Sunday school children coaxed me into sitting in the front seat of a big dipper roller coaster and cascading down the track at a forty-five-degree angle.

I really did not know what to do as I thought if I tried to make a run up the hill to the service road the Beings would target me with some laser and pull me aboard for a 'picnic' of sorts: main course picking Michael's brain and probing Michael's body orifices.

The craft just hovered for a while and then began moving back into the tree cover, slowly, silently knowing that they had been found out by me as I assumed was their thinking. And the very second the last of the craft could be seen by me I ran with the full force that terror can carry a person in emergency situations and I ran for about a mile down the hill, the altitude be damned, I was running for my life.

Part V

You do not want to talk about this.

Let us be real. You are going to a place called HELL after you die. When your spirit is set free of this planet you would wish for a hell. Better than nothing. Floating in space you will find yourself perhaps on some desolate planet: a prison you may not leave; ever. What would your mind do with itself when it has no purpose, no future, just nothing?

And you could not kill yourself. Just emptiness: nothing to do; just exist. Probably no sleep capability. No escape. Just nothingness and your full, complete understanding of the situation. A Hell worse than hell.

No, indeed, you would wish for brimstone rocks, and you working with a wheelbarrow and a shovel, 24-7 times seven, working in a molten quarry having a Hieronymus Bosch creature in real life sticking you with a pike up your butt. And yet, you would agree better than being a wandering star in a very cold universe. At least you would have something to do today. And you might even see someone whom you wished were in hell when you were walking on the top side on planet earth. Oh, that would be a fun one (comic relief at its most sublime):

... "Hey, Jake, you Bastard, hot enough for you? You asshole!"

Part VI

Did you really want to know?

I am talking pedophile. From the gym where I do work-out to the White House in Washington the District of Columbia. Let us not even get started dialoguing Hollywood. But then lets!

And let us start with two of our most favorite directors: Roman Polanski and Woody Allen. Good boys, that is, when talking both directing and acting. Roman: OMG! Brilliant. How does he do it?

Oh, Baby. Rosemary's Baby, the film. How did he set the mood; how did he get the film to work that it was so believable so scary so intriguing? Do you think he had help from the Prince of Darkness? Did He, whisper in Roman's ear, teach Roman special filmmaking skills of overall staging mood and coloring and meter or was Roman already "gifted"? Had Roman's insertion of his penis into the anus of the underage girl, been some sort of quid pro quo of some strange agreement?

Do you remember we talked about the book The Exorcist and how it was so successfully portrayed in the film version? The film Rosemary's Baby and The Exorcist were presented to audiences the world over the same decade, circa 1960's, planet Earth; do you recall?

And then there is Woody. Did he? Would he? And apparently, he did. His own daughter for starters. A kid. A child, and in her adult age giving full testimony to the New York Times. Perhaps there had been others in Woody's life; ya think?

But then Mr. Woody gives secret testimony to the layer of pedophilia in Hollywood when as he and a friend were driving in a car in the movie Annie Hall the friend said he had been 'entertaining' two fourteen year old girls.

And since this is such a topic in the media today and in the halls of government where people are championing the sex slave trade in the United States, I refer you further on to that topic of interest.

Chapter III

Of Aliens and such things.

I first approached the possibility of there being alien beings visiting the planet as do all persons who consume media as a child and as a child considers there being a real Frankenstein monster prowling about. BUT I decided in my early forties to do some investigation into there being real potential for extraterrestrials.

I was in a local library when I saw a book entitled: <u>UFO</u>. I assure you it was a moment of truth when I was considering picking the book off the shelf and as I walked back and forth in front of the book pretending, in the event there might be someone watching, that I was not in the throes of extraterrestrial quandary and simply scanning the shelves. I knew inherently that if I began reading this book, I would be giving myself over to an entire topic that seemed very weird.

And yet I am a curious lad and so I read the flap written by the author to see if I could find fault with the subject and yet I did find that the man who wrote the book was an astrophysicist. It was his captivating testimony that he was not trying to sell the reader on any idea and that he was simply stating what he knew to be true and this was the reason I checked the book out.

The one thing I do remember him writing was that in full view of over one hundred people in New York city a woman was yes, pulled from the window of her apartment residence by a beam of light and taken up into a space craft.

I think the definitive book on UFO etc., is Jim Marrs book <u>Alien Agenda</u>. This will spoil a surprise for you if you choose to read Jim's book when you learn that an alien craft did crash in a Midwest town in America in the late 1800's. Creature Beings were pulled from the craft and planted in the local cemetery. The newspaper headline referencing this is reprinted in Marrs' book. Oh, my!

I find it fascinating that when I began to date Caroline that I did not know her father was world famous rocket inventor. I would tell my friends I was dating a new person and when one of them asked her last name I told them it was Goddard and this person said "Not Robert Goddard?"

I responded "Who b' dat?"

You see, it is all destiny. Here is the gentleman who basically invented Area 51 with his rocket experiments (catch him on you tube in a business suit with his assistants hauling rockets out into the desert by hand) and his daughter becomes a signpost that my grandmother handing me that book many years before was really proclaiming a prophecy. Oh, my!

Oh, and just for fun In one of Jim Marrs books, <u>PSI Spies,</u> he talks about Dr. Tyler's interdimensional PSI spies and how one the spies thought just for fun they should wear masks that looked like the then President Ronald Regan so when the Soviet spies met them in the sky ether they would think Uncle Ronnie was able to go interdimensional too! Yuck, Yuck, Yuri and Boris!

Etc.:

Chapter IV

Circle back.

It is the Jewish Bible not the Old Testament. How many years have Jews had to suffer silently in a Protestant/Catholic society as every mention of The Bible in public discourse has been referred to The Old and New Testament? Let Jews have their privacies and their beliefs and their culture but please be a convert like me that I recognize the Jews want nothing to do with Jesus Christ and their sacred book of Abraham, Isaac, Moses is the Jewish Bible.

And when I was a child of say, nine, I was talking with Mr. Weise in the receiving hall of his and his wife's home. It was Hanukkah and this very liberal Jewish family, up from LA, had a large Christmas tree with presents displayed in their living room.

My mother had gone looking for me through the house and when she came into the hall Mr. Weise and I were having a spirited conversation about Judaism and when my mother approached us I turned to her and said "Mother, I want to become Jewish!"

Oh, the dynamic. Christmas tree and wrapped gifts, the seasons of two religions intersecting and my Mother Italian, Roman Catholic. Without a flicker of hesitation My mother bent at the waist and with her then, in style bright red lipstick and a large smile said "Yes", indeed an emphatic yes. Seems her little boy had found religion for himself.

And yet nothing came of this decision of mine. I remember going to Temple a few times and to Jewish festivals, and several wakes but I never converted. Lucky for the Jews.

And speaking of one of the most exotic, incredulous stories of the Jewish scriptures perhaps *the* most incredulous story, Voila! Ladies, Gentlemen, Alien Beings of all the known universe may I present to you: The Book of Daniel chapter ten.

Oh yes, we have all heard of Daniel in the lion's den, where God of the Jews shut the lions mouths as Daniel the prophet was lowered into the pit by order/decree of king Nebuchadnezzar of the Babylonians. Well, hast thou heard of the time the angel Gabriel was in inflight to kibitz with Daniel the prophet and did proclaim that he had been hindered by the prince of Persia!?

No big eh? Read this again: "I would have come to thee sooner (Daniel) but I was in the midst of a war with the prince of Persia."

Oh, I get it. So, this arch angel of the universe, known and unknown to humankind, had to fight (and was in the middle of a thirty-day fight with whom?). Yes, none other than the prince of Persia.

And who is the prince of Persia? Well, three guesses. If Gabriel is from the God of Heaven who might God's archangel be fighting thirty days?

Correct. And have you ever heard of one Rabbi teaching this story to his congregation? NO. Not this year or anytime soon I am thinking. Too religious for today's modernism.

Chapter V

Thanks, Bill, Thanks Mrs. Gates!

I became the biggest fan of William Henry Gates III when the United States State Department sat him down to question him/ accuse himself and Microsoft of monopolizing the PC market.

Although the jargon of torts was so very far upon and above me, I did not follow all the technical bantering between Mr. Gates and the courts. And yet!.... the one thing I did remember is that one publication had an illustration/cartoon of Bill, wearing boxing gloves, shoes and shorts, in his boxing corner, beaten bloodied but with a smile on his face. He had won. Against the full armada of the British navy, oh sorry, against the full depositional force of the United States court system, William Henry Gates III won. Hurrah!

And now onto the very difficult part of our story. Part II

Part II: -Gates is not People

Did you know the Protestant religion is the one great religion of the planet and that we have the atheist William Henry Gates III for his defining contribution of this definitive argument?

Way to go Bill!

Do you recall the Bill and the Melinda Gates foundation? Ah yes, that incredible outreach to persons of the planet in need of the basic gifts of nature that he himself, William Henry Gates III and his beautiful, wonderful help meet had been blessed with?

Yes. Fine effort; excellent motives. We love you Gates Foundation! Bless Thee!

And yet the experiment was a failure as admitted to by William Henry Gates III. Nice try.

And yet, it was perhaps the most incredible testimony to my claims about Protestantism that could have verified themselves coming from the camps of The Humanistic, Atheistic religions.

Let us let those steeped in sociological verse fight out the above statement among themselves.

For the little people such as you and me we are satisfied by simple explanations for complex problems.

And quite simply the flat map presented on the home page of Gates Foundation detailed all 195 countries of planet earth and how every country was colored in either shale grey or a soft blue. The countries designated by The Gates Foundation as being 'underdeveloped' were colored in the grey. All the other countries (twelve altogether) colored in blue were Protestant nations and noted to be 'advanced'. Period.

I was challenged that Japan was colored blue. But I remembered that Japan had had 400 years of both Catholic and Protestant evangelization. So, Japan should be colored blue/grey? And then there was Israel. I consider Israel one of the most advanced nations on the planet. So, Gates does not consider Israel a nation?

For me I am a lowly janitor so as I said I qualify as a 'little people'. And yet for me a big thought that I carry is that the defining mark of any religion or culture is how women are treated. Are they honored, cherished and equal?

And what of slavery. Not until John Witherspoon of England, a Protestant preacher, did anyone movement begin…. ever, that railed against the sin of human slavery. Was its John or was it his understanding of the human soul via the teachings of the Protestant church that he concluded that all persons have souls and therefore inherent worth?

If rumors are not, and what I have been told is true, the likes of Gates and the They Are Not People crowd have a well mapped plan internationally to eliminate great swaths of humanity. I have heard from Frankie who in his native dark skin says the first and most targeted people for murder are those who are of dark complexion. They will be eliminated first by Gates and friends to make the world a more hospitable place for those who are not people.

Oh for sure there will be plenty of hair cut people, even janitors, those to keep the mechanics of the earth working, electricians, doctors, inventors, astronauts, and a lot of sex slaves: bare bottom boys and bare butt girls.

This new certified slave collection of sex toys will be Nordic in color of hair, blue of eyes and Nordic in body structure. In short, they who have given themselves to follow demonic activities will follow Adolph Hitler's plan of growing an Aryan race. Perfect blond hair, blue eyed beauties. And in time as robotic AI children are manufactured to the point of being non distinguishable counterparts of the Aryans those breathing oxygen instead of cyber electricity will be murdered as well.

Well, well, welcome to hell.

Now, you must admit this concept of eternal punishment for the human soul in the confines of a Hieronymus Bosch landscape is a fitting reward for those who are not...etc.?

Chapter VI

In the Out Door

I began practicing transcendental meditation at age seventeen. I had at the time begun to watch on television Richard Hittleman, a yoga instructor from his Los Angeles studio. At the same time there was Lilias from Seattle, a lovely yogi and very patient and encouraging to her television students. There was no such thing as a Pilates or yoga studio in Sacramento at the time as opposed to today there is one or the other on every corner or the street.

The first time I practiced T.M. I did go out of body. It is curious and fun to watch yourself from a perch twelve feet up in the air as you watch yourself meditating. I have had very few other T. M. experiences. I did not see the need for them.

I have had bouts of astral projection so called but I have never been able to make an inanimate object move just by looking at it and focusing my mind on the object as my mentor Cal could. The first time you see something move by mind power alone you think this must be a trick as your entire life has not been fitted to know such a thing.

Cal was a thirty-second-degree Free Mason and I was introduced to him by his son via a screen writing class we were both attending.

Once I told his son that I was a painter of the fine arts he introduced me to Cal whom in his earlier career had been the head of the art studio of Universal Pictures and by hand, would paint in landscape scenes for big screen movies that are still aired today.

'And when the student is ready the teacher will appear' is the excellent saying that was played out in my life as I had had all the fine art oil painting experience I needed save for one, and this would be the science of color, mixing and applying them to a canvas. And yet, somewhere in my training with Cal, a man I had adopted as surrogate father, I realized that color was more religion than just pure science.

Here we go again with the spirit world which if you are a practitioner of this art then you see that within the color spectrum there is an infinite number of color combinations and color hues. And this is something that I had understood as a child in that each color to me represented a sound of musical notation. This is not an uncommon knowledge of savants and there is a grand name attached to it. And yet even though I did have this insight as I wrote, I did not have telekinetic abilities as did Cal.

I would be sitting at my easel in Cal's studio and he would sit on my right side and instruct me on the mixtures of colors. And it was that first time that he trusted me enough to observe his controlling of a physical object when a paint tube cap started gliding slowly across the table where my color mixing palette was.

I was startled, as I said, and my mind immediately tried to convince itself that either the table was slanted unevenly or that there was some sort of magnetic trick being played. And then I looked at Cal and saw that he was staring at the paint cap. I then looked again at the cap that was still in motion and then looked back at Cal who was still staring at the object. "Keep painting, Mikey," he said without looking at me. And I did continue painting.

And I was wanting and, I was even jealous of Cal's "talent" and often when alone tried moving things by concentration alone. Cal or I never talked about his ability of telekinesis as there is in the ether world a quiet understanding that some subjects are sacred and never to be talked of.

But in my day, I was quite capable of putting my hand or finger on playing cards face down and able to read the card exactly of its suit, its numerical worth and the color. No big. And in those days, I was in love with Tanya, a clairvoyant from Ukraine and being hooked up with such a person I believe I was all the more able to tap into the 'other side'.

One day, Tanya who was living three hundred miles away from me was driving in the mountains and stopped to get gasoline and noticed her left tire was nearly without air. She called me from the gas station and asked "Why didn't you tell me my tire was flat?" I hesitated a minute feeling very guilty and said "I am sorry, it is just that I did not know if it was your right or left tire." For you see in my Western thinking mind, I often did not trust my own conversations with the other side. Rather as the cone in your eye perceives things upside down and then pictures that thing for you right side up, so to, as you are looking through the ether you question your own perceptions.

Man, women! You can go for long romantic walks on the beach, kiss passionately one another, give gifts, proclaim love but just try not telling them their rear tire is flat. Man, will you be in trouble!

Part II

One of my university professors said 'The world is one great tragedy with a few television commercials thrown in, so we all don't go mad'. And it is a wonder we have not all gone mad here on planet earth. There are those who really have gone off the rails for one reason or another, and I think many times those are persons who have given up trying and opt for the easy way of life, letting the State tell you when you can and cannot poop in the morning.

For myself I could easily have gone off the psychic rail many times in life but just decided to move along and forward having faith that everything given you can be endured. For people who give up I think we should put them permanently on The Farm.

And the farm in this atmosphere should be the template the Jews have designed for their society and this is the Kibbutz. Yes, let us give these persons who have shot drugs into their veins for fun and frolic for so many years and now expect me with my tax dollars to take care of them, permanently we the community say "No".

Give them the choice: jail or the Kibbutz. Believe me they will all choose the Kibbutz. No loitering, no pan handling, work, and more work!

Today is your day to make beds. Tomorrow the gardens. The day after the kitchen; cooking, cleaning, serving and yes, food.

And let us not forget there are thousands who would visit your special K and help you amp up your skills so you might become employable. For myself I would teach reading, writing, fine arts, social skills, turn you onto the best books. So, what are we waiting for!

But no more this insanity of catering to the lifestyle of the lost and lazy. What of it? A warm bed, clean showering. Solid food. You have a problem with this? The Kibbutz or jail; good for the druggie good for society.

Amen.

Part III

You must understand the level of hatred of religion before you read further. Understand.

I renounced my Christianity at one time. I told God "You leave me alone; I will leave you alone!"

And yet my spirit craved still a relation of love and I steeped myself into what is termed The New Age Movement. My, what a bag of tricks this religion is. So many egos to placate, so many authors trying out for the lecture tour. The fame of it all.

I was involved with Tanya at this time and we wandered together down the house of mirrored hallways tasting this guru's foods and then moved others. Alien encounters were the rage and Tanya and I would drive to remote landscapes to do 'remote viewing' as we snuggled together in a sleeping bag on the flat bed of my truck. This viewing is an attempt to connect with Beings Alien visa telepathically. Ah, and alas we never quite connected. And yet at one seminar we did encounter Emotive Children, all dressed in all white gowns by their adorning parental guardians. These children could read with their hands and their feet magazine, books, and news articles given randomly by the audience participants. Some could even read by putting printed materials up under their arm pits.

Oh, my.

Many friends, one God:

Girls,

Both sisters were one more beautiful than the other. And I fantasized about marrying either one and becoming a convert to their Muslim religion. And that we were at desert one day, all three of us, these two highly polished, well groomed, intelligent and kindly children of God, when I asked them if they would consider going back to live the lives of true Princess in Arabia and they, as if by electrical switch which had been tapped, swung their heads from side to side "No".

Boys,

Mark Collins whom I affectionately call "The nice Jewish boy, up from Los Angeles" was the one to come to my apartment after the police office told me on the phone that my daughter was dead and that I should go to a friend's house that night or invite someone over to visit with me. Mark drove to my apartment in light speed time and he and I read Psalms 23 from his fine, Jewish bible. He also told me at some later date that he wished all white people were dead while at the same time tapping my hand assuring me, everyone but myself.

Part IV

Of pandemics and men:

Perhaps I have not emphasized greatly enough the spirit world that surrounds us. I like the description in the book The Great Gatsby, where Nick talks about that foul dust, that unseen mist that surrounded and preyed upon Mr. Gatsby.

So to the dust that does surround us all of planet earth; astronomers of our day say it is the 'empty space' or 'dark matter' which is filled with all things moving interdimensional such as the Prince of Persia as I have stated above.

And so too for those Who Are Not People, they are surrounded by dust, an evil dust and move in conjunction with its purpose not knowing, as Jesus said "what they are doing", to the great delight of those who should not be named. These frail individuals who will one day stop breathing having been the useful fools to cause egregious horrors upon humanity for which they too must eventually pay the Piper. For it is the Piper who calls, and it is He who allows you to play your little games for which you will eternally own.

Chapter VII

In the days gone by

Vihn had escaped the reeducation camps of Vietnam where he had lived once, the United States had pulled out from the Vietnam landscape and left the communists of China to move in and to take control of the land and people.

There in the camps Vihn and his friends were taught the virtues of Mao and learned to sing praise songs to him. He did have the experience of watching his best friend taken from the hut in which they were sleeping one night, and the communist soldiers took the young man outside and put a gun barrel to his skull. Vihn recounted that his friend's entire head turned to slush, and his brains and skull exploded upon the wall to which he was standing.

It would be the last time I would see Vihn as we had our regular meal of dim sum which he had introduced to me and Vietnamese coffee. He was going to live with his brothers in another city and we assured each other that we would keep in touch by letter.

Vihn looked at me in our very few last moments together and put his index finger on my temple and said: "I know your mind, you are Buddhist." Perhaps.

In the name of the Father, the Son, the Holy Ghost.

The end.

Appendices:

'Authors' note: I had waited three years to write this story; I knew it was coming and yet stories do take their own time to formulate in your mind and soul. I did understand that the story would not actually begin to be written until something gelled me. Was it to be a physical accident? A lost love. Something?.... I was open and waiting.

And then They Are Not People decided to scare all of the little people with a flu virus and that very day there was proclaimed a lock-down on Sacramento, the city that does not support my art, and I called Lou and we walked a very long walk along the levy by his house and he addressed my pent up anxieties and calmed my nerves with logic and as always salted his conversation with several real time stories that related to traumas and their conclusions of persons he had known or read about.

That evening when I arrived home after cleaning urinals, I began writing the script you have above you. (I washed and sanitized my hands first.)

The End

www.ingramcontent.com/pod-product-compliance
Lightning Source LLC
Chambersburg PA
CBHW070746240726
48654CB00010B/1183